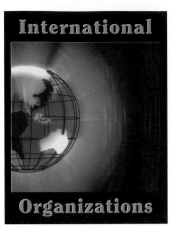

World Health Organization

Deborah A. Grahame

WORLD ALMANAC® LIBRARY

Please visit our web site at: www.worldalmanaclibrary.com
For a free color catalog describing World Almanac® Library's list
of high-quality books and multimedia programs, call 1-800-848-2928 (USA)
or 1-800-387-3178 (Canada). World Almanac® Library's fax: (414) 332-3567.

Library of Congress Cataloging-in-Publication Data

Grahame, Deborah A.
    World Health Organization / by Deborah A. Grahame.
        p. cm. — (International organizations)
    Summary: Describes the founding, development, and staffing of the World Health Organization, and
its focus on immunization, disease prevention, sanitation, and nutrition as well as combating disease.
    Includes bibliographical references and index.
    ISBN 0-8368-5524-8 (lib. bdg.)
    ISBN 0-8368-5533-7 (softcover)
    1. World Health Organization—History. 2. World Health—Juvenile literature. 3. Public health—
International cooperation—Juvenile literature. [1. World Health Organization.] I. Title.
    II. International organizations (Milwaukee, Wis.)
    RA441.G73   2003
    610'.6'01—dc21   2003047996

First published in 2004 by
World Almanac® Library
330 West Olive Street, Suite 100
Milwaukee, WI 53212 USA

Copyright © 2004 by World Almanac® Library.

Developed by Books Two, Inc.
Editor: Jean B. Black
Design and Maps: Krueger Graphics, Inc.: Karla J. Krueger and Victoria L. Buck
Indexer: Chandelle Black
World Almanac® Library editor: JoAnn Early Macken
World Almanac® Library art direction: Tammy Gruenewald

Photo Credits: All photos Copyright World Health Organization/P. VIROT, except the following:
Agricultural Research Service: 37; © AP Photo/Pavel Rahman: 29; © CICR: 27; © CICR/BARRY,
Jessica: 16; © International Federation of the Red Cross/Viet Thanh: 18; Library of Congress: 21;
© Louise Gubb/CORBIS SABA: 32; © Massimo Mastrorillo/CORBIS: 36; Pan American Health
Organization: 7, 30, 39; United Nations Photo Library: 25, 34

Printed in the United States of America

1 2 3 4 5 6 7 8 9 07 06 05 04 03

TABLE OF CONTENTS

Words that appear in the glossary are printed in
boldface type the first time they occur in the text.

Chapter One

Fighters for Health

"Where have you hidden the dead rats?" This strange question is asked regularly of the children living today in the villages of Madagascar, Africa. The children there have become important helpers in the fight against a deadly disease—plague, once known as the Black Death. Rats spread this disease by carrying around the fleas that are infected with plague. The children show local health workers where people dispose of dead rats. Many villagers are afraid to help the health workers in their efforts to end plague. They believe, mistakenly, that the workers will perform medical experiments on the bodies of dead family members. The villagers also fear that the workers will prevent the bodies from having a proper burial.

WHO is Here to Help

Plague is still present today throughout Africa, Asia, and the Americas. The World Health Organization (WHO) has called it "a re-emerging disease." In 1999, fourteen countries reported more than 2,500 cases of plague to WHO. Since its founding in 1948 as a Specialized Agency of the United Nations, WHO has created programs to wipe out diseases such as plague, smallpox, measles, malaria, and cholera. This organization works in dozens of countries throughout the world to help people achieve and maintain the highest level of good health.

WHO's constitution defines health as "a state of complete physical, mental and social well-being and not merely the absence of disease or infirmity." This means there is much more to being healthy than simply not

New Threat of an Old Disease

Stories about the plague seem to belong only in the pages of a history book, but the disease is making headlines today in many parts of the world. During the Middle Ages, this disease, called the Black Death, wiped out one-third of the people living in Europe. Plague struck again in London during the seventeenth century. Early in the twentieth century, the disease claimed the lives of millions of Native people of the Americas.

In the twenty-first century, world travelers visiting remote areas step back in time in more ways than one. Plague is back, and it remains a deadly threat.

being sick. WHO's programs focus on several key areas that affect people's health:

- **Vaccines** and **immunization**
- Disease prevention and treatment
- Mother and child health
- Environmental sanitation
- Nutrition

The organization also works to promote cooperation among scientists and researchers. It helps governments of many countries improve the health services available to their people. WHO's top priorities include childhood immunization, safe drinking water, and prevention of disease. It is playing a major role in helping the people in developing countries live safer, healthier lives.

How WHO Began

The history of the World Health Organization is rooted in the expansion of travel and trade. Progress in transportation exploded during the Industrial Revolution, which had spread from England throughout Europe and to the United States by the early to mid-nineteenth century. Steamships and railways allowed goods and people to move efficiently from place to place. This progress was not entirely

Some diseases, such as tuberculosis, are spread throughout the world. These men in Ethiopia carried a patient with tuberculosis.

An Unfair Exchange

When people from Europe first arrived in North America, they brought new ideas and goods to help build the "New World." They also brought diseases such as cholera, measles, and smallpox. Native American people did not have **immune systems** prepared to fight these diseases. Their traditional herbal medicines did not provide cures. Native American populations dropped from ten million to one or two million, and some tribes were entirely wiped out.

positive, however. Diseases in isolated parts of the world began to spread, traveling as far and wide as people and their goods.

By the early decades of the 1800s, diseases such as cholera reached Europe from the East. **Epidemics** of cholera in 1830 and 1847 killed many thousands throughout Europe. In response, doctors organized the first International Sanitary Conference, which met in Paris in 1851. This conference was not effective in helping to fight cholera because too little was known about the disease or how it spread. The meetings did plant the seeds for cooperation among international health experts.

WHO evolved from health organizations that had been formed early in the twentieth century. Epidemics of cholera, smallpox, and typhus were the common concerns of these groups. The first global health organization was the Pan American Health Organization (PAHO), established in Washington, D.C., in 1902. It was originally known as the International Sanitary Bureau. In Europe, *L'Office International d'Hygiène Publique* was established in 1908. In Geneva, Switzerland, the League of Nations began the International Health Organization of the League of Nations in 1919. The International Sanitary Conference continued to meet until 1938. At this time, Europe was on the brink of World War II. The world and its global health issues were about to change forever.

World War II (1939–1945) was fought throughout the world. The war killed about fifty million people and left great destruction in many countries. Leaders of the world wanted to be sure this kind of war never happened again. They called for the creation of a unified international group that would pledge to keep peace among nations. The meetings these leaders held led to the creation of the United Nations in 1945.

The UN's New Health Organization

In 1945, immediately after World War II ended, the UN voted to establish an international health organization. It approved the constitution of the World Health Organization in 1946. Over the next two years, WHO took over the work of *L'Office International d'Hygiène Publique* and the International Health Organization. The Pan American Health Organization became one of WHO's regional offices.

The Pan American Health Organization existed long before WHO and celebrated its one-hundredth birthday in 2002. This exhibit was at its headquarters in Washington, D.C.

WHO works with other UN agencies, such as the United Nations Children's Fund (UNICEF), the Food and Agriculture Organization (FAO), and the United Nations Educational, Scientific and Cultural Organization (UNESCO). It also works directly with national governments, NGOs (nongovernment organizations), businesses, and individuals.

Members of WHO must accept WHO's constitution. Most members are also members of the United Nations. Other countries may apply for membership in WHO and are admitted by majority vote of WHO's policy-making group, the World Health Assembly. WHO has 192 member nations. Only the Cook Islands and Niue are not also among the 191

The World Health Assembly meets once each year at its headquarters in Geneva, Switzerland, and makes policy for WHO. This picture was taken at the 2002 Assembly.

members of the UN. Leichtenstein has status as an "observer" instead of as a full member.

The organization has two major sources of funding. WHO's regular budget comes from dues paid by its member countries. There is a two-year budget period. The regular budget has been frozen at $800 million per budget period since 1980. The freeze occurred because several member states declared that they were unable to pay their dues. Donor countries provide the main source of the organization's money, which amounts to $1.4 billion per budget period. These voluntary donations make up two-thirds of WHO's total budget. Other UN organizations and private individuals also donate funds to WHO.

The Structure of WHO

The 192 member nations of WHO that make up the World Health Assembly decide WHO's policies, budget, and programs. This group meets in May each year at world headquarters in Geneva, Switzerland, close to the headquarters of many of the organizations related to the United Nations.

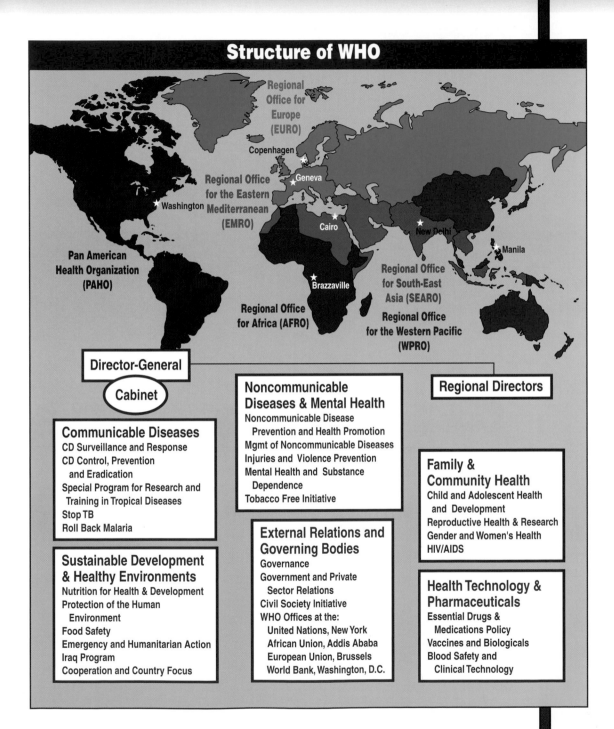

Structure of WHO

Regional Office for Europe (EURO)

Copenhagen

Geneva

Regional Office for the Eastern Mediterranean (EMRO)

Washington

Cairo

New Delhi

Manila

Pan American Health Organization (PAHO)

Brazzaville

Regional Office for South-East Asia (SEARO)

Regional Office for Africa (AFRO)

Regional Office for the Western Pacific (WPRO)

Director-General

Cabinet

Regional Directors

Communicable Diseases
CD Surveillance and Response
CD Control, Prevention
 and Eradication
Special Program for Research and
 Training in Tropical Diseases
Stop TB
Roll Back Malaria

Noncommunicable Diseases & Mental Health
Noncommunicable Disease
 Prevention and Health Promotion
Mgmt of Noncommunicable Diseases
Injuries and Violence Prevention
Mental Health and Substance
 Dependence
Tobacco Free Initiative

Family & Community Health
Child and Adolescent Health
 and Development
Reproductive Health & Research
Gender and Women's Health
HIV/AIDS

Sustainable Development & Healthy Environments
Nutrition for Health & Development
Protection of the Human
 Environment
Food Safety
Emergency and Humanitarian Action
Iraq Program
Cooperation and Country Focus

External Relations and Governing Bodies
Governance
Government and Private
 Sector Relations
Civil Society Initiative
WHO Offices at the:
 United Nations, New York
 African Union, Addis Ababa
 European Union, Brussels
 World Bank, Washington, D.C.

Health Technology & Pharmaceuticals
Essential Drugs &
 Medications Policy
Vaccines and Biologicals
Blood Safety and
 Clinical Technology

The headquarters of the World Health Organization is located in Geneva, Switzerland.

WHO's Executive Board represents thirty-two member countries. Each country chooses a delegate to the Executive Board who is qualified in some area of the health field. Delegates are elected for three-year terms, and the Board meets each year in January. Members prepare and approve the Assembly's agenda for its annual May meeting. The Board advises the Health Assembly and helps it accomplish its goals.

The Secretariat carries out the missions and policies decided by the World Health Assembly. It handles the administrative matters, or paperwork, of the organization. It has a staff of about 3,500 experts and support staff working in headquarters and regional offices as well as in other countries. The leader of the Secretariat is the director-general, who is nominated by the Executive Board. The director-general acts as the president or chief executive of the organization. Member countries elect the director-general for a term of five years. The director-general from

1998 to 2003 was Dr. Gro Harlem Brundtland, the former prime minister of Norway and a prominent environmentalist. She was succeeded in 2003 by Dr. Jong Wook Lee of South Korea. Dr. Lee had worked for WHO for almost twenty years and had most recently been head of WHO's tuberculosis program.

In 2003, Dr. Gro Harlem Brundtland (left) of Norway was followed as director-general of WHO by Dr. Jong-Wook Lee of South Korea (right).

WHO's Principles

The Preamble to the constitution of the World Health Organization declares that the following principles are "basic to the happiness, harmonious relations and security of all peoples:

Health is the state of complete physical, mental and social well-being and not merely the absence of disease or infirmity.

The enjoyment of the highest attainable standard of health is one of the fundamental rights of every human being without distinction of race, religion, political belief, economic or social condition.

The health of all peoples is fundamental to the attainment of peace and security and is dependent upon the fullest cooperation of individuals and States.

The achievement of any State in the promotion and protection of health is of value to all.

Unequal development in different countries in the promotion of health and control of disease, especially communicable disease, is a common danger.

Healthy development of the child is of basic importance; the ability to live harmoniously in a changing total environment is essential to such development.

The extension to all peoples of the benefits of medical, psychological and related knowledge is essential to the fullest attainment of health.

Informed opinion and active cooperation on the part of the public are of the utmost importance in the improvement of the health of the people.

Governments have a responsibility for the health of their peoples, which can be fulfilled only by the provision of adequate health and social measures."

Victory Through Vaccines

Smallpox has left its ugly mark on history for thousands of years. Historians believe pharaoh Ramses V of ancient Egypt died of the disease because they found smallpox scars remaining on his mummy. In Hernan Cortés's military conquest of the ancient Aztec capital, Tenochtitlán, in Mexico, he and his conquistadors unintentionally brought another form of warfare—smallpox—to the Aztec people. The disease also traveled west with America's pioneers.

A **virus** called *Variola major* causes smallpox. It is transmitted by air from person to person by a cough or sneeze. In about ten days, an infected person suffers high fever and muscle aches. About two or three days after that, a rash of small pustules develops on the face and spreads to other parts of the body. The disease is very contagious and can be fatal.

Lady Mary Montagu, wife of a British ambassador to the Ottoman Empire, saw that the Turkish people deliberately put smallpox pus into a wound on a healthy person to keep that person from becoming ill. The principle behind this curious practice proved to be medically sound. Working on this principle, British physician Edward Jenner created a smallpox vaccine, the world's first vaccine. He carried out his first experiments on humans in 1796.

WHO has come close to completely eliminating smallpox, which can cause the terrible pus-filled bumps called pustules seen on this baby photographed many years ago.

One of WHO's earliest priorities was a campaign against smallpox launched in 1958. The campaign had amazing success. The last case of smallpox was confirmed in 1977 in Somalia. By 1980, routine smallpox vaccinations ended. Smallpox was **eradicated**, or completely wiped out, worldwide. It is the first disease eliminated from nature by science.

Mass Vaccinations

By the end of the nineteenth century, scientists understood much about how vaccines prevent disease. Vaccines against smallpox and rabies were available by the 1890s. By the end of the 1920s, people could be vaccinated for diphtheria, tetanus, tuberculosis (TB), and pertussis (whooping cough).

Smallpox: Take Two?

Bioterrorism is a real concern today. A bioterrorist act involves the intentional use of diseases or chemical agents to hurt perhaps thousands of people. Harmful germs and chemicals could be released into the air or water supplies. Diseases such as smallpox could be used as weapons of war. When smallpox was eradicated before 1980, WHO recommended that laboratories destroy their stocks of the virus. It also advised Russia and the United States to safeguard any remaining stocks. Russia used the stocks to create biological weapons before agreeing to end this practice.

In November 2002, U.S. President George W. Bush called for health officials to keep samples of the smallpox virus secure. In this way, it will be available for research as well as for reacting to any bioterrorist threat to people in the United States. Vaccines became available to health-care workers in the winter of 2002–03.

Vaccines were not in widespread use right away, however. During the 1930s and 1940s, outbreaks of diseases preventable by vaccine still occurred. After World War II, many more new vaccines were developed, including vaccines for polio and measles. At that time, the brand-new World Health Organization began programs of mass immunization.

WHO has plans to wipe out other diseases through its immunization programs. By 2005, the organization expects to eradicate polio by concentrating on vaccination in what they call reservoir countries, where high populations, high birth rates, and low routine immunization rates allow the disease to stay active. These countries are Bangladesh, India, the Democratic Republic of the Congo, Ethiopia, Nigeria, and Pakistan.

A volunteer posted a notice In New Delhi, India, about a mass vaccination program against polio.

The Push Against Polio

A virus that causes poliomyelitis, or polio, enters the body through the nose or mouth. It attacks nerve cells of the brain and spinal cord. Early symptoms include neck and back stiffness. Muscles weaken until the victim cannot stand or walk. The disease can lead to partial or total lifelong paralysis. The disease was formerly called infantile paralysis because it was thought to attack only children.

During the 1950s, American researchers Jonas E. Salk and Albert Sabin developed vaccines against polio. The Salk vaccine, approved for use in 1955, is an injection. The Sabin vaccine, approved in 1962, is taken orally, or by mouth. The vaccines have greatly reduced this fearsome disease in developing countries.

Childhood Immunization

In the United States and Canada, vaccination is an important part of a "well baby" check-up. Babies are immunized against DTP (diphtheria-tetanus-pertussis), poliomyelitis, and MMR (measles, mumps, and rubella). A child cannot enter school until these immunizations are complete and up to date.

In 1974, WHO began a program to wipe out those same childhood diseases through worldwide vaccination. Succeeding at such challenges has required help from other public and private groups.

The Cycle of Neglect

Many children in developing countries today do not have access to vaccines. For example, in sub-Saharan Africa, only about half of children are immunized during their first year of life. In recent years, a cycle of neglect has acted as a barrier between these children and vaccines.

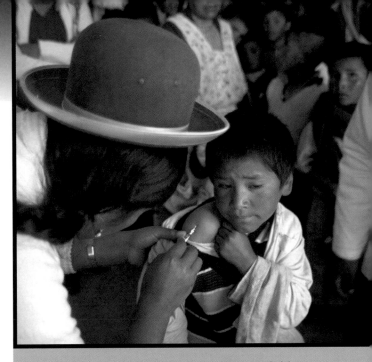

A medical team administers vaccinations to children in a South American Indian community, bringing them a lifetime of protection from certain diseases.

The cycle is complex. Politicians and doctors have not been emphasizing the importance of vaccination in developing countries. As a result, there has been little new research and development of new vaccines. Therefore, drug companies have sharply reduced production of vaccines. When vaccine supplies are low, vaccine prices go up. Fewer of the expensive vaccines can be purchased for developing nations with WHO's funds. When fewer vaccines are purchased, vaccine production slows even more. In addition to these problems, poor roads and lack of vehicles in good repair threaten the ability to deliver vaccines. Medical staff in these countries may be poorly trained. Vaccine equipment may not be kept sterile. Needles may not be disposed of properly.

A new international group has stopped this cycle of neglect. In 2000, WHO launched the Global Alliance for Vaccines and Immunization (GAVI). WHO's GAVI partners include UNICEF, the World Bank Group, and the Bill and Melinda Gates Foundation. The group funded vaccination programs in Afghanistan, China, India, Sierra Leone, Liberia, and Indonesia.

The health of the inhabitants of the Gaza Strip was a continuing problem in 2002 when their villages were being destroyed by Israeli troops.

A Vaccine Crisis for Palestinians

Conflict between Palestinians and Israelis has been on the increase. More than 2,520 Palestinians and 625 Israelis were killed in 2001 and 2002 alone. This conflict has caused a health crisis for Palestinians. Many Palestinians in remote areas have no access to vaccines. There are delays in transporting the vaccines to these areas. Frequent cuts in electrical power affect vaccine refrigerators. Malnutrition is common, especially for children. More babies die before birth as a result of poor health care for pregnant women. Water and sanitation systems are damaged.

WHO's World Health Assembly called upon its director-general to visit the Palestinian territories. Israel has not been willing to allow access to these places, however, because Israel does not agree that Palestinians' health problems are serious enough for WHO's concern.

Outbreaks and Epidemics

Achy muscles, high fever, sore throat, extreme fatigue—sound familiar? Welcome to flu season! The most widely spread contagious disease in North America is also the most talked about—influenza, or flu for short. Many people of all ages have had bouts with flu. Flu tends to strike in winter, which means epidemics occur at different times of the year around the world. The flu virus is constantly changing, so last year's vaccine may not be effective against this year's strain of flu.

Flu is a respiratory illness that is transmitted by coughing and sneezing. Complications can include pneumonia, which claims the lives of many elderly and very young people. The "Spanish Flu" pandemic, or global epidemic, occurred between 1918 and 1920 and killed at least twenty million people.

Today, WHO continues the influenza program it began in 1948. WHO conducts a worldwide influenza watch in eighty-three countries. It established an international network to develop ways to diagnose flu. The network's goals also include ways to control the spread and severity of flu. Each year, WHO reviews the flu virus strains in circulation and recommends the ingredients for the next season's flu shot. This recommendation is then passed on to vaccine manufacturers.

Epidemics

From its earliest days, WHO worked to prevent and control diseases such as yaws (a painful skin condition), malaria, **venereal diseases**, leprosy, and trachoma (a serious

The Mystery of SARS

WHO doesn't just deal with known diseases in known populations. In 2003, a mysterious respiratory disease began to spread from China. Given the name SARS (for severe acute respiratory syndrome), it was carried by people traveling by air until it reached cities worldwide. WHO quickly had scientists investigating the illness—where it started, how it spreads, whether people can pass on the disease before they have symptoms, which victims are most likely to die, whether it helps to **quarantine** a victim, and so on. WHO warned people not to travel if they weren't feeling good because they might be passing the illness on. In the meantime, WHO's scientists worked with researchers the world over to find ways to treat and prevent the disease.

On the Trail of Cholera

When the U.S. Congress passed the Indian Removal Act in 1830, several tribes were forced to leave their homes in the Southeast and move west. Along with bitter cold and exhaustion suffered by the people, an outbreak of cholera struck. Many people died of the disease. The Cherokees' forced march under the U.S. Army at this time is known as the "Trail of Tears."

Cholera also traveled along the Oregon Trail. People used the 2,000-mile (3,200 kilometer) trail across the Rocky Mountains in the 1840s during the Westward Expansion until 1869, when the railroad across the United States was developed. The hardship of poor diet and harsh weather weakened the settlers on the trail and made them vulnerable to disease. Cholera was one of the main illnesses that people suffered, in addition to smallpox and dysentery.

Cholera is an intestinal illness caused by a bacterium called *Vibrio cholerae*. Cholera is transmitted by water contaminated with human waste from people already infected with the disease. Victims suffer severe loss of body fluids, or dehydration. Shock and death can follow. Doctors treat cholera by giving the patient plenty of specially formulated liquids to replace the lost fluids. The disease can be prevented by keeping water supplies clean. Cholera is often a major problem after a natural disaster that harms a community's water supply. In this photo, when floods ravaged Vietnam in 2000, people were surrounded by water, but they had no water that was safe to drink, so cholera became a threat.

eye condition). During the 1960s, WHO brought a major epidemic of yellow fever under control in Africa. It also helped control an outbreak of cholera in Asia and the Western Pacific at that time.

Today, the three major **infectious** diseases that threaten people in developing countries are malaria, tuberculosis, and human immunodeficiency **virus**/acquired immunodeficiency syndrome (HIV/AIDS). These three diseases cause more than three hundred million illnesses and five million deaths each year. Besides the human cost in lives lost, infectious diseases cost developing countries in other ways. These diseases contribute to political, social, and economic insecurity as well as hurting agricultural and industrial growth. Developing countries cannot prosper and grow unless their people are physically well.

WHO is planning actions that will cut in half the number of deaths caused by TB and malaria. Deaths from HIV/AIDS can be reduced by 25 percent. As part of the solution, WHO proposes to focus on mass education for the people about ways to prevent these diseases. For malaria prevention, WHO makes mosquito nets widely available. **Condoms** must also be made more available for HIV/AIDS prevention. Wealthier nations and groups in partnership with WHO will need to commit funds directly for these projects.

Malaria, which is common in tropical regions, is caused by single-celled **parasites** called *Plasmodia*. These parasites are spread by the bite of female mosquitoes. The *Plasmodia* multiply rapidly in the liver, and when they are released, they cause red blood cells to rupture. It is estimated that in Africa alone, 2,800 children die every day of malaria.

The first of WHO's major efforts against disease was the fight against malaria. In the 1950s, malaria killed two hundred million people each year. After World War II, DDT spray was used to wipe out the mosquitoes that carried malaria. Use of this spray had its problems, however. People in many countries involved, including Vietnam, Thailand, Iran, and the Philippines, were **nomadic**. They moved around according to the season. Spraying the walls of their houses was not effective because nomadic peoples often lived in makeshift huts with hardly any walls. Also, DDT was found to be very harmful to the environment.

In 1955, WHO launched the Malaria Eradication Program (MEP). Through the years, this program had some major setbacks. Health workers were not well trained, program costs rose, and funds were drastically reduced. In addition to the environmental problems caused by DDT spraying, DDT supplies were often limited. To make matters worse,

Even a simple method such as soaking the netting that goes around a bed with insecticide can help prevent malaria. This is one of the methods taught in WHO's Roll Back Malaria campaign.

mosquitoes became resistant to DDT and other insecticides. The *Plasmodia* parasites developed resistance to drugs.

Malaria still claims the lives of more than three thousand people each day. WHO has launched a new campaign against the disease, the Roll Back Malaria campaign, with partners from both public and private organizations. Its aim is to cut the deaths from malaria in half by 2010.

The plague, or Black Death, devastated the people of medieval Europe. Tuberculosis, an infectious disease of the lungs, is often called the "white plague" because of the shockingly pale appearance of its victims. Past generations called the disease "consumption" because it seemed to consume, or eat up, its victims.

Rod-shaped bacteria called *Tubercle bacilli* cause the disease. A cough, similar to one that accompanies a cold, is often an early symptom. There may be blood in the fluids brought up if there is damage to the lung. Later stages of the disease include such symptoms as chest pain, weight loss, night sweats, and fatigue. TB commonly attacks older people and infants as well as those suffering from AIDS and from malnutrition. These groups are at a higher risk for contracting TB because their immune systems are not strong.

During the 1800s, most TB victims were kept isolated in sanitariums, special rest centers, for months or even years to allow their bodies to fight the disease and to keep the disease from spreading. Today, drugs that stop the bacteria from multiplying are used.

TB is still a deadly threat on several continents. Health experts have identified twenty-two countries as the worst affected, including Brazil, China, Pakistan, South Africa, and Vietnam. In Nigeria and Thailand, TB and HIV exist together as a co-epidemic. WHO's goal is to accomplish TB control worldwide by 2005.

The Lifestyle Diseases

Cancer, diabetes, and cardiovascular (heart and blood vessel) disease are known as lifestyle diseases. They can occur as a result of choices made in life. WHO supports programs that help people make healthy choices about exercise, diet, and smoking.

There are one billion smokers in the world today. Four million people die each year as a result of cigarette smoking. By the year 2020, that number is expected to reach 8.4 million. A recent WHO study revealed that cigarettes are becoming cheaper in developing countries, making it easier for people to afford cigarettes and smoke more. Seventy percent of

During the 1918 influenza pandemic, this French poster said, "The other danger. Let us not rest on our laurels. Tuberculosis threatens us. It must be defeated." The deadly disease still has not been completely wiped out.

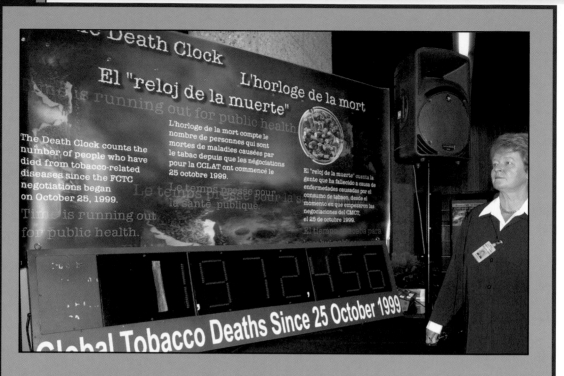

The Tobacco Free Initiative

WHO launched a campaign called the Tobacco Free Initiative in October 2000 to make the public aware of the tobacco health crisis. This campaign resulted in WHO's first international treaty. The treaty is called the Framework Convention on Tobacco Control. Member states that sign this treaty promise to work toward reducing use of tobacco in their countries. Some opponents of this initiative think that WHO has no business interfering in a commercial enterprise such as tobacco manufacture and sales. The photo shows Director-General Brundtland at an exhibit in WHO headquarters in Geneva that estimated the number of people who died of tobacco-related diseases.

those deaths are likely to occur in many of these countries where programs for tobacco control are weak—Costa Rica, Côte d'Ivoire (Ivory Coast), and Vietnam, for example. WHO recommends that taxes on tobacco be greatly increased to slow the rate at which people pick up the smoking habit. High cigarette prices often make people cut down on smoking or quit the habit.

HIV/AIDS

In the late 1970s, people in the United States and Sweden began to die from a strange, unidentified condition. By 1982, the condition was being given a name: acquired immunodeficiency syndrome, or AIDS. At first, it was thought to be restricted to homosexual men. Then researchers realized that everyone could be vulnerable to this deadly disease through sexual contact or through tainted blood supplies. It was discovered that people first get a virus called human immunodeficiency virus, or HIV. Victims may not come down with AIDS until long after acquiring the virus, and many become ill with diseases and conditions associated with HIV. The disease name has now been changed to HIV/AIDS.

Forty-two million people now live with HIV/AIDS. The vast majority—95 percent— live in low- or middle- income countries. In 2002, 3.1 million people worldwide died of AIDS. Since 1996, a new drug treatment has been used to greatly reduce the number of HIV-related illnesses and deaths. These drugs are costly and not widely available in the countries that

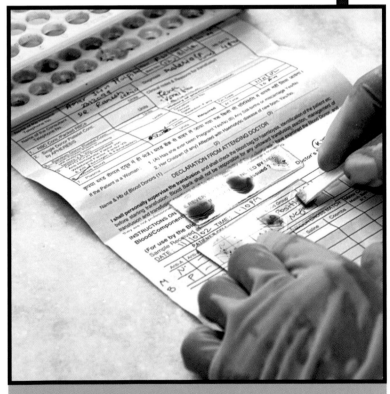

This HIV test was carried out in India. It is estimated that the number of deaths from HIV/AIDS in India is approaching half a million a year.

need them the most.

In December 2002, WHO formed a new alliance to focus on this problem: the International HIV Treatment Access **Coalition** (ITAC). Within this group, WHO is working with more than fifty partners to make drug treatment available in countries such as Botswana, Costa Rica, Cuba, and Nigeria.

War: Bad for Your Health

War in Afghanistan has been a reality for years. It has left the twenty-seven million people of Afghanistan in poverty and poor health. Life expectancy there is forty-six years of age (compared to almost seventy-seven in the United States). Six million Afghans have no access to health care. Each year, malaria and TB kill more than half a million Afghans, and sixteen thousand women die from causes related to pregnancy.

WHO is working with the Afghan Ministry of Health to correct this situation. Along with its partners, such as UNICEF and nongovernmental organizations, WHO has asked for donations of $129 million. With these funds, WHO can develop a health system for the country and also support refugees in countries surrounding Afghanistan.

In January 2003, a pertussis (whooping cough) outbreak struck parts of northeastern Afghanistan. Health officials estimated that the lives of forty thousand children who had never been vaccinated for pertussis were threatened by the disease. WHO worked with other UN agencies and the country's Ministry of Health to deliver the antibiotic drug erythromycin to treat children and mothers.

WHO views war as a global health issue. This means that when countries go to war, health services for civilian, or nonmilitary, people are put at risk. After many years of war, the Iraqi people have a serious health and economic crisis. **Sanctions** imposed on the country since 1990 led to shortages of food and medicine. As Operation Iraqi Freedom swept dictator Saddam Hussein from power in 2003, widespread looting of equipment and loss of electricity and water-treatment plants added to the country's woes.

The director of WHO's Iraq Program immediately began to gain support for rebuilding Iraq's health system, which involves making sure Iraq's water and sanitation systems are quickly put into good working order throughout the country. The program also involves continued attention to basic medical services, such as vaccination campaigns. WHO and its partners pledged to support rebuilding and **humanitarian** aid in Afghanistan and Iraq.

Violence and Health

Each day, 4,400 people worldwide die as a result

Many people in Afghanistan have had to abandon their homes and seek safety away from ongoing wars. Such refugees are in danger from many health problems.

WHO volunteers often use dancers, singers, and drama to get people to pay attention to a health campaign that will benefit them. This dancer was part of a campaign in Africa.

of violence. Thousands more survive but are changed by violence—as victims, witnesses, or family members of victims. The idea of connecting violent behavior and public health concerns is a new one in many countries. WHO has defined health as "a complete state of well-being." Violence clearly does not promote well-being. Victims of violence may need emergency and long-term health-care services. Child abuse and neglect are forms of violence. Physical violence in families, neglect of senior citizens, and youth violence threaten the well-being of individuals as well as of society.

WHO declared violence a major public health issue in 1996. To support this declaration, in 2002, WHO launched a Global Campaign on Violence Prevention. At the same time, the organization released its first report on the subject, the *World Report on Violence and Health.* Its main purpose is to prompt authorities the world over to explore methods of prevention.

Certain high-risk behaviors, such as the use of alcohol and drugs, are associated with violence. Access to guns is another factor. WHO's report notes that there are environmental, social, and behavioral factors related to violence. Alternatives to violence should be available. Preventing violence means getting communities involved. Communities need to be concerned with family counseling, parenting classes, and social and sports activities.

Primary Health Care for All

Primary health care is basic health care that everyone should receive in order to prevent major illnesses and make sure that they are strong and well. Millions of people in the world do not receive primary health care. In 1978, WHO adopted the Declaration of Alma-Ata, which was the result of an international conference on primary health care held in Alma-Ata, Russia (the former Soviet Union). The declaration called on governments to put primary health care at the core of their national health systems. It also called for health care for all by the year 2000.

The goal was not met, which has been a disappointment. WHO and its partners are studying this failure and considering new strategies.

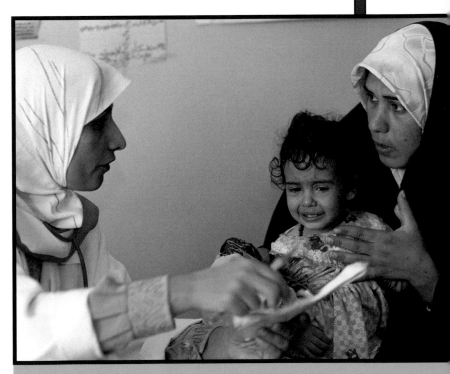

Primary health care begins even before the birth of a baby. This mother in Iraq brought her toddler to an international clinic to check out her health and to have her vaccinated.

Gender Matters

This girl in Ethiopia may face a painful and difficult future because of the cultural practice of female genital mutilation. This practice takes place throughout Africa and is cultural in origin, not religious.

Women are the heads of their households in about one-third of the homes in developing countries. They are educators, mothers, farmers, workers, and community leaders. Women make up about one-half the world's population. Despite the important roles women play, women and girls still experience inequality and abuse in some cultures.

The Girl Child

In many places, boy babies are highly desired. If a girl baby is born, she may be abandoned, left outside to starve or die of exposure. This practice is called female infanticide. In China, couples are allowed to have only one child, and most couples want boys. Female infanticide often takes place in China and in other parts of Asia.

In some parts of the world, girls are still discriminated against just because they are female. For example, girls have fewer opportunities to get a good education. They are kept at home to do chores while boys go to school. Young girls can be taken from their families and forced into marriage or even into **prostitution**.

In some cultures, a practice known as female genital mutilation (FGM) is common. Cutting the private parts of girls' bodies this way is a form of abuse. There is no medical or religious reason for this practice. It is a painful act with a long history that robs girls of their dignity and makes them feel ashamed to be female. The practice is common in African and Eastern Mediterranean regions. It also is known to take place among some immigrant populations in the United States and Canada. Many people around the world have spoken out against this form of mutilation.

WHO is working to develop training materials for health workers in areas where FGM is common. WHO sponsors workshops to help nurses and midwives become aware of the medical and psychological problems related to this procedure.

Violence Against Women

Violence against women and girls is common in some parts of the world, such as the Middle East and the South Asian nations of India, Bangladesh, and Pakistan. In these cultures, women are seen as inferior to men and as merely property designed to please men and serve the family. A woman's behavior as a daughter, wife, and mother defines her worth. "**Honor killing**" is an ancient custom in these places. This crime is acceptable to many in the culture if a man feels that his wife's actions dishonor him or his family.

Acid violence is another crime against women. A man throws acid on a woman so that her skin is

These women from Bangladesh were disfigured by acid attacks. They had plastic surgery in Spain to repair the worst of the damage to their faces.

burned, and she is disfigured for life. This is a punishment for a woman who fails to please a man or his family in some way. Her disfigurement is a warning to other women to be obedient and submissive to men. In Bangladesh, 200 acid attacks were reported between 1996 and 1998.

Cruel violence against women is considered normal in some cultures, and is even considered a man's right. For example, while cooking dinner, a wife may be killed by an exploding kitchen stove. Behind this "planned accident," called "bride burning," is a husband who is unhappy with his bride's dowry, or the money he received from her parents. About five thousand women in India are killed in similar ways each year.

Since 1996, WHO officials have been speaking out against violence against women. They say that women who experience violence in their lives suffer a higher proportion of ill health than women who live violence-free lives.

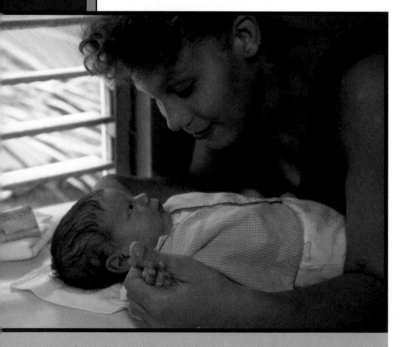

Mothers the world over seek ways to give their babies the strongest start in life. WHO supports breastfeeding babies.

Off to a Good Start

The World Health Organization cares for mothers and their babies by helping women to have safer childbirths and to choose effective family planning methods. WHO also supports mothers who want to breastfeed their infants. Many nutrition experts believe that breastfeeding is an infant's best start in life because breast milk naturally strengthens the baby's immune system. The baby is protected from many diseases that are common in poor areas of the world.

In many parts of the world, though, breastfeeding is frowned on as too old-fashioned in these "modern" times. Many mothers want to feed their infants formula, which is artificial milk that is given through a bottle. Feeding infant formula to babies in developing countries is not always in the babies' best interest. Poor mothers might not know how to correctly mix the formula powder with water. They may use unsafe water instead of boiled water. They may use too much water in order to make the expensive powder last longer. Living conditions in poor areas are often dirty. If the bottles and feeding equipment are not kept clean, the baby can get sick.

In developed countries, though, feeding infants formula is a safe alternative to breast-feeding because there is a clean water supply, and mothers are likely to use the formula correctly. Children in developed countries also have better access to medical care.

In the United States and Europe, 20 percent of adult HIV infections occur in women. That number rises to 30 percent in Asia and 55 percent in sub-Saharan Africa. Each year, half a million HIV infections occur in children under age fifteen, mostly transmitted from their mothers.

Worldwide, women are more likely than men to be infected with the HIV virus. If a woman has an untreated venereal disease, her risk of being infected with HIV increases. In developing countries, women are often blamed for spreading HIV. Women are financially dependent on men, and some must trade sexual favors for their survival and that of

> ### It's in the Blood
>
> Women and children are the main recipients of blood transfusions. A woman may need to be given a new supply of blood during or after the birth of a baby. WHO aims to reduce the need for transfusions by increasing the mother's quality of nutrition during pregnancy. WHO also supports efforts to screen blood for purity and safety. Safe blood means blood that is used for transfusions is screened for the HIV virus and other diseases. In developing countries, such screening sometimes does not take place.

their children. In some cultures, it is acceptable for men to have several sex partners. This increases the chance of the spread of HIV.

WHO supports education programs that promote the use of male and female condoms. These are usually the only protection methods available. Even though they are often distributed free, their use is low. In some societies, if a woman insists that a man use a condom, she is suspected of being unfaithful. WHO and its partners have much work ahead to help change such ideas. These women need more power and equality in their relationships and control of their health and their lives.

If a mother knows she is HIV-positive, she may breastfeed during her baby's first few months and later switch to formula. Breastfeeding is recommended because its health benefits outweigh the risk of passing HIV infection through breast milk. If a woman does not know whether she is HIV-positive, she is still encouraged to breastfeed, because bottle-feeding can be risky. Babies becoming sick on poorly mixed formula is still a bigger health risk than HIV from mother's milk. WHO recommends that an HIV-positive mother be counseled about her own circumstances and given the support she needs in making a final decision about feeding her infant.

Students in Zambia performed cultural songs and dances to raise awareness of AIDS among their peers. In Zambia alone, more than one million children have been orphaned by AIDS.

A Healthy Environment

Water is the key to health and life, but it also can be the source of disease and even death. Bacteria, human or animal waste, or insects that carry disease may pollute water. Dirty water and poor personal cleaning habits increase chances for disease. Having clean, safe water means families can have water for drinking, washing their clothes, taking baths, and keeping their homes cleaner.

In times of war, **drought**, and famine, safe drinking water and sanitation can be at risk. Sanitation means removing human and animal waste and keeping water supplies clean. People living in places without clean water can

For many people the world over, acquiring a daily supply of fresh, safe water is a major activity of everyday life. This woman in northeastern Africa must carry heavy loads of water home.

be exposed to diseases such as cholera. A simple disorder such as diarrhea, which can be spread in unsafe water, can be life threatening because the body loses so much fluid it becomes dehydrated.

Lack of rain for long periods of time causes natural water supplies, such as lakes and streams, to dry up. The result is drought. Water supplies can become stagnant and full of bacteria. Crops fail to grow because the soil is too dry. People have less food as well as less clean water. Starvation and disease follow.

In Ethiopia, poor rains during the spring of 2002 led to a widespread drought. Food shortages and lack of clean water put hundreds of thousands of people at risk of hunger, sickness, and even death. Deadly droughts occur with terrible regularity in Africa.

Drought has always been a problem in many parts of Africa. Today, it is being made worse by global warming because the climate of the whole world is changing. Areas near the Sahara Desert are becoming sandier every year.

Lack of clean air and water harm all living creatures, especially young children. According to WHO studies, children under the age of five suffer 40 percent of the diseases linked to environmental problems. Pesticide spraying, lead from gasoline, and toxic chemicals released from factories cause air pollution. Chemicals and pesticides may pollute water as well.

Changes in the environment, such as deterioration of the ozone layer around Earth, global warming, and the destruction of natural resources, also pose health risks. In May 2002, WHO joined with UNICEF and the UN Environmental Program to publish facts about these problems in a report called *Children in the New Millennium: Environmental Impact on Health.* Reports by agencies such as these bring world attention to the problem and spark discussions about finding solutions.

Ethiopia's prime minister asked the world to help his country overcome the drought of 2002, and governments of Norway, Sweden, and the Netherlands donated funds to help WHO respond to the crisis. As a result, WHO was able to send 164 Emergency Health Kits to Ethiopia. Each kit contains one ton of medicines, supplies, and instruments for helping about ten thousand people. Millions of people benefit from Emergency Health Kits.

The international health community is concerned about safe drinking water and child health. WHO and Ethiopia's Ministry of Health have joined forces to make sure feeding programs are running properly. Together, they have launched programs for distributing measles vaccines and vitamin A supplements. WHO also helps the country fix its water supply systems. WHO and the country's Ministry of Health train health workers in environmental sanitation methods.

Lack of safe drinking water can lead to dracunculiasis, also known as guinea worm disease. It is a serious disease caused by a parasitic worm, but it is preventable by simple means: filtering, digging wells, and providing hand pumps. Between 1980 and 2000, the occurrence of this disease decreased by 98 percent—the world was almost free of it. Then, armed conflict, such as that in Sudan, destroyed good water sources, resurrecting this disease in Africa. In 2001, sixty thousand cases of the disease were reported. Eleven other countries have also recorded cases.

Dry areas, such as this one in Ethiopia, may only have a few working wells. Women must wait long hours for a turn to fill their water jugs.

The Carter Center has joined WHO and UNICEF in efforts to end the disease. At a March 2002 meeting in Sudan, former U.S. President Jimmy Carter called for "financial support, political will, and diplomatic backing" so that affected countries could get back to water safety quickly.

Asia's Hazards to Health

Heavy traffic in Asian cities such as Bangkok can create lasting problems for children who grow up inhaling the lead from polluted air.

Asia's environment is suffering because it has become industrialized very quickly but without the safeguards that many countries now use to protect the air and water. Asia does not use lead-free gasoline in its cars as Europe and the United States do. Car exhaust there contains lead from petroleum. Children are especially at risk. High levels of lead in their blood can result in learning disabilities.

The problem is serious because more than half of the world's people live in Asia. Children make up about 40 percent of the Asian population. WHO is monitoring Asia's air and water pollution problems. At a meeting in Bangkok, Thailand, in March 2002, health and environmental experts advised Asia to switch to lead-free petroleum.

Asia also faces other modern hazards to its environment. Factories dump untreated waste into rivers and canals. People use this water for bathing and cooking. Pesticides used in farming expose crops and livestock to toxic chemicals.

Of Food and Famine

At five years old, Ahmed was bright-eyed and laughed easily. Just seven weeks earlier, he had to be carried to the feeding center in his mother's arms. He weighed only 33 pounds (15 kilograms), and he was so weak he couldn't move. He gained 10 pounds (4.5 kilograms) as a result of care at the feeding center.

Ahmed lives in Ethiopia, where a drought has lasted for more than three years. Skeletons of cattle and sheep litter the dry fields. There is no clean water to mix the children's porridge. Some families walk for days to large towns in search of feeding centers. They flee their homes in remote regions where wells have dried up, crops have withered, and camels have stopped giving milk. Some children become so weakened by the journey that they die before the eyes of relief officials.

Malnutrition—Why?

There is no lack of food in the world today. Agricultural production increased markedly during the past century. Farming techniques and equipment became highly efficient. Why are so many people hungry and malnourished? The problem is not a lack of food but a lack of equity, or fairness, about how the food is distributed. The land is fertile and crops are abundant in poor countries. Greed causes landowners to export the food for cash. Not enough food is left behind to feed the people who live where the land is not good.

Taking into account the entire world, food supplies are out of balance. Some nations have plenty; others often suffer famine.

The results are overabundance and even considerable waste in a few parts of the world and shortages, hunger, and famine in many other parts.

WHO considers malnutrition "the single most important risk factor for disease." One of every three people worldwide is malnourished. Malnutrition is more than a matter of not getting enough food. It leaves the body weak and prone to infections. Malnutrition is also more than a medical problem. Its roots are found in poverty and discrimination. Better nutrition leads to better health. Better health means a strong immune system that can fight off diseases.

This child in India does not get enough of the right food to grow properly. She may suffer the effects her whole life.

Hunger is Happening Today

Hunger affects one in seven people on Earth each day. In Somalia, for example, war keeps food from getting to half a million starving people. Drought is also a factor. WHO and UNICEF distribute high-protein biscuits and specially treated milk to thousands of Somali children each year. War, floods, earthquakes, and hurricanes can lead to times of famine. Poverty causes many millions of children to have little or nothing to eat. Thousands of children still starve to death each year.

Fourteen million people in the Horn of Africa (Ethiopia,

Somalia, and Eritrea) spent most of 2002 in severe need of food and water. Only a year before, WHO and other relief organizations had joined forces to prevent a famine in that region. A famine was avoided in 2001, but about 40 percent of people living in the Horn are still malnourished. Another famine could occur at any time.

Famine in southern Africa affects several countries already devastated by HIV/AIDS. These six countries—Lesotho, Malawi, Mozambique, Swaziland, Zambia, and Zimbabwe—are made up of mostly farming communities. The impact of the disease in these communities is felt not only as sickness but also as hunger. Members of farm households and farm laborers who suffer from the disease cannot plant and harvest crops

Living Large

Not only famine but also an overabundance of food can cause a health crisis. Many chronic diseases are associated with fatty diets, high cholesterol, poor dietary habits, and lack of physical activity. Cardiovascular disease, adult-onset diabetes, stroke, cancers, and **obesity** are facts of life in wealthy countries. These diseases were once referred to as "rich men's diseases." Now they are also on the rise in developing countries. The worldwide trend toward unhealthy weight gain and its related diseases has a new name: "globesity." Globesity increases the health burdens upon developing countries already struggling to control infectious diseases.

Vegetables are available in some markets throughout Africa, but they are not eaten often enough to improve most people's health.

as efficiently. When crop output drops, household income also drops. People cannot buy much food. Weakness from HIV-related illness has diminished people's ability to survive the famine. In 2001, about five hundred thousand people in these six countries died of AIDS. Many left behind children too young to farm the land.

WHO and the UN Program on HIV/AIDS (UNAIDS) released a joint report in 2002 explaining how this famine fuels the HIV epidemic. The conclusion of the report calls for an increase in global awareness and financial assistance to end the cycle of hunger and death.

The "5 A Day" Way

Do Americans eat a total of five fruits and vegetables each day? How about even two a day? Adding fruits and vegetables to one's daily diet helps prevent chronic diseases. It also fills in nutritional gaps and builds resistance to infectious diseases. The 5 A Day International Symposium, held in Berlin, Germany, in January 2003, focused on increasing the worldwide consumption of fruits and vegetables. In most countries of the world, these foods are not part of the typical daily diet, yet scientists know these foods are important to a healthy diet. The problem is convincing people to change.

The 5 A Day program is the largest nutrition education program in the United States. The symposium, held every two years, gives representatives from several countries an opportunity to share ideas about turning this poor nutrition trend around. WHO expects that an increase in consumer demand for vegetables and fruits will have an impact on global food production as well as on world health.

Food Safety

Health experts have made a strong link between food safety and public health. WHO works to ensure that food supplies are safe by calling together public health experts to examine ways to protect people from contaminants such as pesticides as well as salmonella and other bacteria. In developing countries, contaminated food has caused many of the deaths of children under age five. Mothers often prepare infant food in the morning for the entire day. By nightfall, the food is full of bacteria. In developed nations, people who eat contaminated chicken or milk products can become sick with food poisoning.

People who eat steak and other beef products must take care to avoid beef infected with bovine spongiform encephalopathy (BSE). BSE, called "mad cow disease," affects the brain and spinal cord of cattle, causing them to behave strangely. This new, rare disease is a challenge to scientists and health experts. When humans develop this disease from infected beef, it is called Creutzfeldt-Jacob disease. The disease first appeared in 1986 in Great Britain. Ten years later, a new strain linked to BSE was discovered. People who raise cattle often feed their cattle a protein-rich meal made from recycled carcasses of cattle, sheep, and goats. This practice has been linked to the spread of the disease. WHO has recommended banning the use of these feeds in all countries and has published guidelines for BSE control.

WHO Looks Ahead

Since the 1990s, the World Health Organization has been an organization in crisis. The agency has been ailing while attempting to face new health challenges worldwide.

In recent years, WHO has been criticized for lack of direction and poor leadership. Its six regional offices were not well connected with each other or with WHO headquarters. The offices did not have much influence in the countries they were committed to serve. They competed with each other for funds from donations. Donors lost confidence and sent much of their money to other agencies, especially the World Bank. Disagreements arose about how much voice donors should have in how the money was spent.

New leadership in July 1998 signaled sweeping changes for WHO. Dr. Gro Harlem Brundtland, the new director-general, started new campaigns that restored the confidence of donors in WHO's agenda, but problems remained throughout her time of leadership, 1998 to 2003. Throughout Dr. Brundtland's term, WHO carried on its important work despite the problems.

In 2003, a new director-general, Dr. Jong-Wook Lee, a native of South Korea, took over. The future of Dr. Brundtland's reforms was no longer clearly in view. Staff morale was low, and negative feelings within the organization had hurt its effectiveness. Competition from other international health organizations had weakened WHO's impact on global health. Many looked to the new regime to pump fresh life into WHO.

In *World Health Report 2000*, for the first time, WHO used eight different measurements to rank countries on the basis of health services available to their citizens. The rankings were severely criticized around the world. Many people thought that WHO had gone beyond its mandate, or the reason it was established.

WHO thought the organization was starting out on a beneficial path. An editorial in the January 2003 issue of the *Bulletin of the World Health Organization* said, "A clear path for WHO would be to continue the

development of the process that [*World Health Report 2000*] started. . . .
Eventually, this process could lead to a codification of the rights of
citizens in relation to the health services. . . . The code on health rights
would complement other developments in human rights legislation,
both in general and as it applies to the specific rights of children, women
and other vulnerable groups."

New Ideas about Traditional Medicine

Traditional medicine differs from modern, or conventional, medicine in
that it makes use of herbal remedies and practices that have existed for

hundreds, even thousands, of years.
Examples are the use of shark cartilage
for strengthening joints and slowing the
growth of tumors; ginger root for colds,
flu, headache, motion sickness, arthritis,
and athlete's foot; **acupuncture** for
anxiety, depression, travel sickness,
and asthma; aromatherapy for headache,
insomnia, lower backache, osteoarthri-
tis, heart disease, and cancer; and yoga
for toning internal muscles and improving flexibility of joints and ligaments.

WHO's regional director for Africa
has noted that about 80 percent of
African people use traditional medicine.
WHO has advised these countries about
ways to make sure alternative medicines
are safe and affordable, especially in
poorer areas. Modern or conventional
Western medicine can be misused. The
same is true for traditional medicine.

This African farmer carefully tended herbs
for use in making traditional medicines for
his community.

Make a Date with Health

The World Health Assembly has named certain dates as health awareness days. The goal is to bring the world's attention to important health topics. These days are:

January 26: World Leprosy Day
March 7: International Women's Day
March 24: World TB Day
April 7: World Health Day
May 31: World No Tobacco Day
Early August: World Breastfeeding Week
November 25: International Day for the Elimination of Violence Against Women
December 1: World AIDS Day

For example, the herb *ma huang* (also known as ephedra) is used in China to treat symptoms related to the common cold. In the United States, the herb was sold as a weight-loss aid. Long-term use of ephedra by dieters caused deaths, strokes, and heart attacks.

WHO wants to help place traditional medicines into the mainstream. WHO will encourage international health experts to require strict testing and regulation for these medicines. The agency will work to prevent natural remedies from being taken over by major companies for huge profits. According to this strategy, care must also be taken to harvest medicinal plants responsibly.

Health as a Bridge to Peace

In August 1997, WHO started its Health as a Bridge to Peace (HBP) program. The Pan American Health Organization (PAHO) coined this term during the 1980s. HBP involves actual peacemaking activities as well as improving health while reducing violence in society.

WHO conflict-management and peace-building programs have been in place since 1998 in countries troubled by war and war-related crises, such as Afghanistan, Angola, Bosnia, Croatia, Mozambique, and Sri Lanka. Health professionals have learned that in these situations, they have an obligation to create opportunities for peace.

Perhaps today more than ever, peace through health is an idea all health organizations—and all people—can agree on as the most important "Health for All in the 21st Century" strategy.

Time Line

1902 First global health organization, Pan American Health Organization (PAHO), is founded.

1919 League of Nations forms the International Health Organization.

1945 World War II ends. United Nations votes to establish an international health agency.

1946 International Health Conference in New York approves Constitution of the World Health Organization.

1948 First World Health Assembly meets in Geneva.

1955 WHO begins its first mass campaign to fight malaria.

1958 WHO's smallpox immunization campaign is launched.

1960s WHO begins campaigns against leprosy, yaws, syphilis, and trachoma.

1970 WHO focuses on family planning, launching a program of research and training.

1974 WHO sets goal to vaccinate children worldwide against diphtheria, tetanus, pertussis, polio, tuberculosis, and measles.

1978 WHO adopts the Declaration of Alma-Ata. This document calls on governments to make primary health care a central feature.

1987 WHO starts the Safe Motherhood Initiative with the goal of reducing maternal diseases and deaths by 50 percent.

1988 WHO's plan to eradicate poliomyelitis by 2000 begins. (The goal was not met; the new target date is 2005.)

1990s "Lifestyle diseases" such as diabetes and cancer lead WHO to begin programs to promote healthy, smoke-free living.

1992 At the Earth Summit, WHO focuses on health problems related to poor environmental conditions.

1993 The UN and WHO begin a new joint program on HIV/AIDS. This program replaces WHO's Global Program on AIDS.

2001 WHO begins a five-year Polio Eradication Initiative.

2003 WHO serves as the worldwide leader in organizing the fight against the SARS epidemic.

Glossary

acupuncture medical practice using long needles inserted at specific body sites

bioterrorism an attack on people using disease weapons, such as anthrax or smallpox

coalition a temporary alliance, or union, between parties or states

condom a rubberlike sheath for use during sexual intercourse to prevent pregnancy and the spread of HIV/AIDS

drought a long period of dry weather that often leads to crop failure and famine

epidemic a disease affecting many people at the same time

eradicate to destroy or remove something, such as a disease

honor killing a murder carried out by a person who thinks his or her honor has been harmed by the victim

humanitarian promoting human welfare

immune system the body's system that produces chemicals to protect against disease

immunization the process of making someone immune to, or protected from, a disease

infectious able to spread quickly by infection from person to person

nomadic pertaining to people who move from place to place

obesity the condition of being very overweight

parasite an organism that lives on or feeds off of another

prostitution performing sexual acts for money

quarantine the isolation of a person with a disease to prevent its spread

sanctions penalties or punishments imposed by one state to force another state to obey or comply

vaccine a medicine that builds immunity to a specific disease

venereal disease a disease transmitted by sexual contact

virus a simple microorganism that causes infectious diseases but that is not a bacterium

To Find Out More

BOOKS

Powell, Jillian. *World Health Organization.* World Organizations Series. Watts, 2000.

Weaver, Lydia. *Close to Home: A Story of the Polio Epidemic.* Once Upon America Series. Puffin, 1997.

ADDRESS AND WEB SITES

WHO Headquarters
Avenue Appia 20
1211 Geneva 27
Switzerland
www.who.int

WHO Regional Offices
   Africa: www.whoafro.org

   Europe: www.euro.who.int

   South-East Asia: w3.whosea.org

   The Americas/Pan American Health Organization (PAHO):
      www.paho.org

   Eastern Mediterranean: www.emro.who.int

   Western Pacific Region: www.wpro.who.int

Index